ALLIANCES AND AMERICAN NATIONAL SECURITY

Elizabeth Sherwood-Randall

October 2006

*****

The author would like to thank General (Ret.) John Shalikashvili for his partnership at the inception of this monograph, Army Major Raymond A. Kimball for his superb research assistance, and the Carnegie Corporation of New York for providing research support under the auspices of the Carnegie Scholar program.

*****

Comments pertaining to this report are invited and should be forwarded to: Director, Strategic Studies Institute, U.S. Army War College, 122 Forbes Ave, Carlisle, PA 17013-5244.

ISBN 1-58487-261-6

FOREWORD

One of the greatest challenges facing the United States today is the translation of its overwhelming might into effective influence. Traditionally, the United States has leveraged its power through bilateral and multilateral alliances. However, the end of the Cold War and the events of September 11, 2001, have led some policymakers and analysts to question the value of alliances in American foreign and defense policy.

This monograph by Dr. Elizabeth Sherwood-Randall, one of the nation's leading specialists on alliance politics, makes the case that allies are more important than ever to the achievement of U.S. national security goals. She argues that existing American alliances need to be modernized and strengthened, and that new alliances should be established. She also stresses the value of peacetime security cooperation, which builds partnerships that may become alliances. Dr. Sherwood-Randall describes the need to evolve the concept of alliances to fit 21st century security threats that may not be confined to a particular region, such as proliferation of weapons of mass destruction or pandemic disease, and recommends the networking of key American alliance relationships into an "alliance of alliances."

DOUGLAS C. LOVELACE, JR.
Director
Strategic Studies Institute

BIOGRAPHICAL SKETCH OF THE AUTHOR

ELIZABETH SHERWOOD-RANDALL is the Adjunct Senior Fellow for Alliance Relations at the Council on Foreign Relations; a Senior Research Scholar at the Center for International Security and Cooperation at Stanford University; and a Senior Advisor to the Preventive Defense Project, a collaborative venture between Stanford and Harvard that develops innovative policy solutions to national security problems. She is also a 2004 Carnegie Scholar. She served as Deputy Assistant Secretary of Defense for Russia, Ukraine, and Eurasia from 1994-96. She was Associate Director of the Harvard Strengthening Democratic Institutions Project from 1990-93. She has been Chief Foreign Affairs and Defense Policy Advisor to Senator Joseph R. Biden, Jr., and a Guest Scholar in Foreign Policy Studies at the Brookings Institution. Dr. Sherwood-Randall received her B.A. from Harvard College and her D.Phil. in International Relations from Oxford University, where she was a Rhodes Scholar.

SUMMARY

The protection and advancement of the national security interests of the United States requires a greater investment than ever in alliances. In the intensely interconnected security environment of the 21st century, the view that alliances are encumbrances rather than enablers is flawed strategically. Alliances are the antithesis of altruism or passivity. They are a highly self-interested proposition in that they are an essential instrument for advancing American national security. Going forward, the purpose of alliances in U.S. national security policy must be fourfold: To generate capabilities that amplify American power; to create a basis of legitimacy for the exercise of American power; to avert impulses to counterbalance American power; and to steer partners away from strategic apathy or excessive self-reliance.

What does an alliance offer that the United States cannot obtain otherwise? Alliances are binding, durable security commitments between two or more nations. The critical ingredients of a meaningful alliance are the shared recognition of common threats and a pledge to take action to counter them. To forge agreement on threats, an alliance requires ongoing policy consultations that continually set expectations for allied behavior. In light of the unpredictable and amorphous nature of new security challenges, such consultations will be essential instruments of American leadership, especially with regard to building and maintaining consensus on ends and means. To generate the capacity to operate together, an alliance requires sustained preparations for combined action. What distinguishes an alliance from any other kind of cooperative relationship is the existence of interoperable military capabilities that enhance prevention, provide deterrence, and contribute to effective defense. In the past, such action has resided largely in the domain of military cooperation; in the future, it will extend to a much broader set of collaborative activities that only recently have come to be understood as vital to national security.

Alliances can range in their obligations from the most expansive—"an attack on one is an attack on all"—to guarantees that are more limited in ambition. Across all alliances, the ideal is the creation of an entity in which the sum of cooperation between or among the participating states will be greater than the sheer arithmetic addition of the constituent parts. At a minimum, allies are expected to take into consideration the perspectives and interests of their partners as they make foreign and defense policy choices. The first impulse of allies should be to turn to one another for support; the last impulse should be to go without or around an ally, or to oppose and seek to thwart an ally's policy goals actively.

Alliances also create incentives for reaching multinational consensus. In the most effective alliances, participants benefit from a central coordinating mechanism that structures consultations and enables horse trading. Allies do not consider each policy issue narrowly on its own merits, but rather within the broader context of prior shared experience, concomitant items on the current agenda, and longer-term goals. Thus allies constantly are stimulated to consider how their interests dovetail with the interests of their partners in order to maximize support for their own priority initiatives.

The array of alliance relationships that the United States maintains today provides a strong foundation for the exercise of American influence. However, it needs to evolve in several critical dimensions to meet present and future needs. It must acknowledge that some traditional allies no longer depend on the United States for their survival as they did during the Cold War, and that the United States may depend more rather than less on its allies in Europe and Asia to achieve its global goals. Further, in the face of transnational dangers, the United States will need to promote alliances that are defined in broader terms than the classical geographically-based model. Transregional linkages among allies and alliances need to be forged in response to global threats. Finally, effective security cooperation necessitates a much wider embrace of governmental functions. A dense network of interactions will be required to deal with challenges such as proliferation and terrorism, which are less susceptible to traditional military tools and require intimate cooperation across previously "domestic" structures.

Some evidence suggests that a tactical course correction is underway in the second term of the Bush administration. The president and his senior advisors have signaled a renewed appreciation of the utility of partners in pursuing American foreign and defense policy goals. Examples include the transition of responsibility for some sectors of Afghanistan from U.S. forces to NATO forces, a qualified endorsement of the European Union diplomatic approach to addressing the Iranian nuclear program, and continued deference to the six-party process for North Korea. Some bilateral alliance relationships also have been strengthened, most notably ties between Washington and Tokyo, although others, such as the American bond with Turkey, remain severely strained. However, to meet the future requirements of its national security, the United States needs to move beyond case-by-case actions toward the strategic recognition that alliances are a net benefit. Long-term policies must be established to support and grow American alliances.

The United States should pursue an alliance *strategy* that is multifaceted, multilayered, and multi-yeared. This would entail a four-pronged approach: First, to build upon existing bilateral and multilateral alliance institutions, relationships, and capabilities; second, to promote the establishment of stronger ties that might become enduring alliances (both bilaterally and multilaterally) with several key countries and regions; third, to invest in peacetime security cooperation with countries that can be coaxed toward partnership and may in the future be capable of sustaining an alliance relationship; and fourth, to utilize the full spectrum of cooperative international arrangements that complement alliances.

To achieve an enduring sense of common interest and purpose, it will not be sufficient to flex American power and expect others to fall in line. The United States must find ways to transform its power into a magnetic force that draws peoples and nations to its goals. It will not serve American national security interests to disparage multilateralism, nor to abandon the pursuit of enduring ties in the illusory hope that less formal arrangements will provide both flexibility and sustained support. The United States must rebuild its alliances and innovate a new kind of connectivity across countries, institutions, and regions that result in a broadly-based alliance system that is far greater than the sum of its disparate parts. The United States also must remain committed to the nitty-gritty effort to make it possible for foreign forces to operate capably alongside American troops, and to establish mechanisms that permit more effective security cooperation with international institutions and nongovernmental organizations.

ALLIANCES AND AMERICAN
NATIONAL SECURITY

Do Americans know who their allies are? If the United States is attacked, do its citizens know who will stand with them? It is surprisingly difficult to answer these questions with certainty. Should Americans care if they have allies? The United States is the strongest nation on earth, the only standing superpower, and its natural impulse is to assume that it can act unencumbered. Paradoxically, America needs allies because of its overwhelming strengths and the vulnerabilities that lurk in the shadow of such unprecedented national power.

In this era of American predominance, alliances are more compelling than ever. Yet compiling a list of U.S. allies and alliances is a sleuthing game. No definitive policy document or reference book provides a straightforward answer.[1] American citizens largely are unaware or uninformed; for example, in the recent uproar over the potential acquisition by a Dubai company of contracts for management of U.S. ports, many were ignorant of Dubai's status as a long-standing partner providing critical support to American policies in the Persian Gulf. The lack of clarity underscores the fact that policymakers and analysts have failed to think strategically or systematically about the role that alliances should play in American national security in the 21st century. As a consequence, they also have failed to build and sustain the public support necessary for enduring global engagements.

What does an alliance offer that the United States cannot obtain otherwise? Alliances are binding, durable security commitments between two or more nations. The critical ingredients of a meaningful alliance are the shared recognition of common threats and a pledge to take action to counter them. To forge agreement on threats, an alliance requires ongoing policy consultations that continually set expectations for allied behavior. In light of the unpredictable and amorphous nature of new security challenges, such consultations will be essential instruments of American leadership, especially with regard to building and maintaining consensus on ends and means. To generate the capacity to operate together, an alliance requires sustained preparations for combined action. In the past, such action has resided largely in the domain of military cooperation; in the future, it will extend to a much broader set of collaborative activities that only recently have come to be understood as vital to national security.

Alliances can range in their obligations from the most expansive—"an attack on one is an attack on all"—to guarantees that are more limited in ambition. Across all alliances, the ideal is the creation of an entity in which the sum of cooperation between or among the participating states will be greater than the sheer arithmetic addition of the constituent parts. At a minimum, allies are expected to take into consideration the perspectives and interests of their partners as they make foreign and defense policy choices. The first impulse of allies should be to turn to one another for support; the last impulse should be to go without or around an ally, or to oppose and seek to thwart an ally's policy goals actively.

Alliances also create incentives for reaching multinational consensus. In the most effective alliances, participants benefit from a central coordinating mechanism that structures consultations and enables horse trading. Allies do not consider each policy issue narrowly on its own merits, but rather within the broader context of prior shared experience, concomitant items on the current agenda, and longer-term goals. Thus allies are stimulated constantly to consider how their interests dovetail with the interests of their partners in order to maximize support for their own priority initiatives.

It is instructive to contrast an alliance with the current vogue in cooperation: the "coalition of the willing." The two are entirely different organisms with respect to the durability of the commitment and the breadth of cooperation — in an era in which cooperation must go far beyond traditional military definitions. Indeed, the sloppy thinking that has characterized the argument that alliances can be replaced with such impromptu arrangements derives from a failure to recognize one fundamental fact: The capabilities that have been fielded by these groupings (despite their evident shortcomings) have derived almost entirely from underlying alliance commitments that over decades have coordinated national policies and prepared participants to operate together effectively on the battlefield. Recent coalitions of the willing have borrowed from investments made in long-standing alliances without acknowledging their debt.

The differences could not be starker between alliances and coalitions of the willing in terms of value added over time. To borrow from the language of interpersonal relations, an alliance is akin to a long marriage, based on an initial lofty commitment that creates a context of comfort, convenience, and the pooling of resources. It also assures reliability because it sets clear standards about partners' behavior. Although it eventually can be burdened by cyclical irritations, accumulated baggage, and the inevitable inclination to push each others' buttons, the price of exit is high.

A coalition of the willing is more like a summer romance, an intense but fleeting attachment, without any fundamental commitment, beginning with the best of behavior but deteriorating over time, and not infrequently ending in heartbreak. It confers less legitimacy and does not offer the promise of enduring loyalty, leading to a greater inclination on the part of members to "play the field," and resulting in a relatively insecure and unpredictable security environment. Above all, a coalition of the willing forsakes the opportunity to invest over the long term and reap the consequent rewards. Comparing the two options, Ashton B. Carter has written that coalitions of the willing should be judged as "a desperate fallback, not a preferred vehicle for U.S. leadership."[2]

ALLIANCES UNDER SIEGE

Across American history, alliances have occupied a dubious status in the minds of some strategists and practitioners and, indeed, in a segment of public opinion. Beginning with the Founding Fathers, the preference has been to "steer clear of permanent alliances," avoid "entangling alliances," and to enter only into "temporary alliances for extraordinary emergencies."[3] At the time of the establishment of the nation, the world power dynamic was notably different: The Americans were weaker than the Europeans who sought their support, and they feared being implicated in wars that that did not reflect the nascent national interest. But these early admonitions established the template for resistance to binding international commitments that could constrain U.S. freedom of action and drag America into unwanted conflict.

Two centuries later, presidential candidate George W. Bush and his senior policy advisors upheld the enduring legacy of this skepticism about ties that might unduly influence U.S. policy choices. For the team that helped Bush prepare for the presidency, the end of the Cold War informed a world view that heralded the special role of American power and warned against the perils of multilateralism. Within a year of taking office, these perspectives would be sharpened by the requirements of waging war against terrorists who threatened the American homeland.

In early 2000, Bush campaign advisor Condoleeza Rice laid down the marker that America's "remarkable position" must define its global role. "Power matters," she argued, "both the exercise of power by the United States and the ability of others to exercise it." She derided those who are "uncomfortable with the notions of power politics, great powers, and power balances." In a Bush Administration, America would use its unprecedented strength to shape the malleable post-Cold War world consistent with its interests, which will "create conditions that promote freedom, markets, and peace."[4] Ivo Daalder and James Lindsay use the term "hegemonist" to describe this approach, which holds that "America's immense power and willingness to wield it, even over the objections of others, is the key to securing America's interests" in a Hobbesian world.[5]

In rhetoric, the early statements by individuals who would become senior Bush administration national security officials generally were positive about alliances, though usually carefully caveated. Rice acknowledged that American interests "are served by having strong alliances" but added that "multilateral agreements and institutions should not be ends in themselves."[6] She expressed the strongest disdain for those who believe that the legitimate exercise of American power derives from the support of other states or international institutions, concluding that the foreign policy of a Republican administration would "proceed from the firm ground of the national interest, not from the interests of an illusory international community."[7]

The case for assertive leadership of America's alliances, consistent with Rice's view on the privileged role of the United States, was set forth as well. Governor Bush made the case in 1999, emphasizing the guiding role the United States must play in the transatlantic relationship: "For NATO to be strong, cohesive and active, the President must give it consistent direction: on the alliance's purpose; on Europe's need to invest more in defense capabilities; and, when necessary, in military conflict."[8] Paul Wolfowitz outlined a more general theme the following year with a message intended to reach allies as well as adversaries who might choose to distance themselves from U.S. policy: The United States would use its power to reward supporters and punish those who undercut its global goals. Describing the American alliance "vocation," he argued that,

> No Cold War lesson is more important than what can be learned from the remarkable U.S. record in building successful coalitions. This includes lessons about the importance of leadership and what it consists of: not lecturing and posturing and demanding, but demonstrating that your friends will be protected and taken care of, that your enemies will be punished, and that those who refuse to support you will live to regret having done so.[9]

With regard to the specific role of alliances in the arsenal of American power, skepticism was growing in Republican circles about whether they should and/or could continue to play a central role in U.S. foreign policy. Underlying this doubt were emerging questions about whether there would be a sufficient overlap of fundamental interests to sustain alliance commitments and whether future international circumstances would be predictable enough to permit joint threat assessment and agreement on priorities and action.[10]

Furthermore, other kinds of less formal arrangements, such as coalitions of the willing, were gaining in appeal. Such groupings had been promoted during the Clinton administration by the Supreme Allied Commander for Europe General John Shalikashvili, who sought to establish a modality that would allow a self-selecting group of North Atlantic Treaty Organization (NATO) allies to engage in collective military action using Alliance assets but without implicating all members.[11] The intent was to supplement rather than supplant the Alliance framework. Richard Haass subsequently put forth the related concept of "foreign policy by posse," which offered the flexibility of "selected nation states coalescing for narrow tasks or purposes." However, he also noted that,

> the informal coalition approach is not without significant drawbacks. By definition, such groups do not exist before the problem or crisis emerges. They therefore offer no deterrent—although, if formed quickly enough, they can still provide a preventive function. Informal coalitions take time to forge . . . The lack of common equipment, military doctrine, and common experience is likely to limit effectiveness. So, too, will a lack of resources.[12]

With the election of George W. Bush and the events of September 11, 2001 (9/11), many of the principles and perspectives articulated during the campaign would be operationalized. The decision to go to war in Afghanistan to rout the Taliban provided the first case. The administration chose not to accept offers of military assistance from NATO and sought instead to put together a coalition providing specific elements of support for the U.S. operation, such as permission for overflight and basing rights in Central Asia. When urged by a European leader to have lots of consultation and take into account the views of others, Bush asserted that "my belief is the best way that we hold this coalition together is to be clear on your objectives and to be clear that we are determined to achieve them. You hold a coalition together by strong leadership and that's what we intend to provide."[13]

In late 2001, Secretary of Defense Donald Rumsfeld reinforced the message that the United States might not choose to rely on mechanisms built during the Cold War to meet new security challenges, observing on CNN that "The worst thing you can do is to allow a coalition to determine what your mission is . . . It's the mission that determines the coalition."[14] Thus began the effort to establish an ad hoc group of countries willing to fight the war on terror as defined by the United States.

As it sought to build support for the invasion of Iraq over the course of the next 2 years, the administration made policy decisions consistent with the views set forth by leading Republican thinkers in 2000. In addition to its fundamental mistrust of ties that bind American power in pursuit of the interests of others and concern about the potential perfidy of allies and institutions that would not support or might even actively obstruct U.S. policy goals, the Bush team became alarmed about the practical liabilities of relying on others to conduct wars.

Emphasizing the imperative of being nimble and responsive in real time, President Bush announced in 2004 with reference to the United Nations (UN) that "America will never seek a permission slip to defend the security of our country."[15] This resistance to subjecting American national security policy to the scrutiny of an international organization extended to alliances. Looking back on NATO's campaign in Bosnia and Kosovo—the first "hot" war ever fought by the Atlantic Alliance—attention focused increasingly on the cumbersome multinational decisionmaking processes that hampered U.S. diplomatic and military effectiveness.[16] Further, the U.S. military's after-action analysis process pointed up the tactical challenges of operating alongside allies who were not as technologically advanced as American forces, as well as the difficulties of preventing the misuse or abuse of intelligence information in a multinational environment.[17] In the face of daunting new security challenges, the costs of allies seemed to outweigh the benefits. Charles Krauthammer summed up this perspective: "Interests diverge. No use wailing about it. The grand alliances are dead. With a few trusted friends, America must carry on alone."[18]

Some evidence suggests that a tactical course correction is underway in the second term of the Bush administration. The president and his senior advisors have signalled a renewed appreciation of the utility of partners in pursuing American foreign and defense policy goals.[19] Examples include the transition of responsibility for some sectors of Afghanistan from U.S. forces to NATO forces, a qualified endorsement of the European Union (EU) diplomatic approach to addressing the Iranian nuclear program, and continued deference to the six-party process for North Korea. Some bilateral alliance relationships also have been strengthened, most notably ties between Washington and Tokyo, although others, such as the American bond with Turkey, remain severely strained. However, to meet the future requirements of its national security, the United States needs to move beyond case-by-case actions toward the strategic recognition that alliances are a net benefit to it. Long-term policies must be established to support and grow American alliances.

WHAT DOES AMERICA GET FROM ALLIANCES?

In the intensely interconnected security environment of the 21st century, the view that alliances are encumbrances rather than enablers is flawed strategically. Alliances are the antithesis of altruism or passivity: They are a highly self-interested proposition in that they are an essential instrument for advancing American national security. While it is self-evident that the United States should retain the right to defend itself, that old institutions must adapt to changing times and, given that less formal arrangements can make a meaningful security contribution, America's national interests now require a greater investment than ever in alliances. Going forward, the purpose of alliances must be fourfold: To generate capabilities that amplify American power; to create a basis of legitimacy for the exercise of American power; to avert impulses to counterbalance American power; and to steer partners away from strategic apathy or excessive self-reliance.

Generating Capabilities that Amplify American Power.

The Iraq war often is cited as an example of why traditional alliance relationships are no longer required or useful. This is wrong both with respect to Iraq itself as well as with regard to the underlying assumption that Iraq is the most likely model of future conflict. The involvement of some NATO allies on a national basis provided important (though not decisive) military support, and almost entirely depended on the years of doctrinal development, planning, equipping, and training undertaken by NATO members. Further, that the Atlantic Alliance was split over the decision to go to war and that key NATO allies such as France and Germany were unwilling to join in the military campaign ensured that the United States would not have broad multinational support and assistance in the much longer and more costly "post-conflict phase" of the effort.

Even more important, the Iraq war is not likely to be the dominant paradigm for the engagement of U.S. military power in the 21st century. Although being prepared to conduct large-scale warfighting operations against a conventional opponent will remain necessary to enhance deterrence as well as deploy force, many of the threats America will face will not lend themselves to traditional military responses, much less unilateral ones.

The short list of major threats which we can neither prevent nor respond to alone includes attacks by terrorists armed with nuclear and/or biological weapons (making the tragedies in New York, Madrid, Bali, and London look like child's play); widespread proliferation of weapons of mass destruction (WMD) and long-range delivery vehicles, including to nonstate actors who have no return address and therefore cannot be deterred in traditional terms; a growing number of failed states that are perfect petri dishes for extremist groups; and the rise of "new" transnational security challenges such as pandemic disease. It is worthy of note that each of these threats may grow in danger in relation to the growth of another; for example, the proliferation of WMD beyond the current nuclear weapons states makes it much more likely that terrorists will be able to obtain them. In order to act preventively rather than react only after catastrophe, America needs access to an expanded toolkit that fully engages the capabilities of other countries as well as its own. It is hard to imagine any scenario in which the United States can respond effectively to these challenges without the sustained support of allies and partners, as it cannot hermetically seal its borders and cocoon itself within them.

Across history, what has distinguished an alliance from any other kind of cooperative relationship between or among nations is the existence of interoperable military capabilities that enhance prevention, provide deterrence, and—should prevention and deterrence fail—contribute to effective defense. A fully evolved alliance is notable for its capability to undertake combined strategic planning, in which two or more nations' national security establishments conduct threat assessments, anticipate future security needs, and commit to the development and implementation of a common program to meet the requirements generated by this process. Rather than scrambling to coordinate their capabilities in a crisis, allies can count on being prepared to operate alongside one another.

Preparedness in the face of new security threats will require the expansion of strategic planning and coordination of effort across allied governments, involving agencies that previously did not consider themselves essential to national security. The day-to-day business of a meaningful alliance of the future will necessitate the collaboration of national security establishments, not just defense and military establishments. This will involve broader and deeper integrated planning, training, and equipping of personnel — including those that do not belong to departments or ministries of defense — than previously has been achieved. To be fully effective, the United States will need to lead an effort to link agencies of government that have not engaged in sustained multinational collaborative activities and which traditionally have resisted "foreign" access. This is most notable in the need for sharing intelligence and fusing data in real time. Such cooperation is very different from preparing to capture and hold territory in order to plant a victory flag on top of a hill.[20]

In the defense and intelligence domains, America's extraordinary technological prowess presents an additional challenge to the full integration of allied capabilities. It is hard for most militaries to fight alongside American forces.[21] Yet it is not in the American interest for its allies to lack capabilities, to use such a deficit as an excuse not to join in military action, or to be such a burden on the U.S. military that it resists taking allies along (as was the case in Afghanistan in 2001). Thus the United States needs to lead a continuing effort to make such coordination possible, working through established mechanisms provided by its alliance relationships.

Creating a Basis of Legitimacy for the Exercise of American Power.

For the United States, the issue of legitimacy largely was dormant throughout the Cold War. America held the moral high ground; the enemy was repressive domestically and imperialistic abroad. Occasionally it chose to use its power in ways that strained relations with its allies, such as at Suez in 1956 or during the Vietnam War, but never to the breaking point; what held its alliances together was much more compelling than whatever centrifugal forces might be at work.

In the aftermath of three seminal events — November 9, 1989 (11/9, the fall of the Berlin Wall and what it presaged: the collapse of the Soviet Union and the Warsaw Pact); 9/11; and the decision by the Bush administration to resort to preventive war in Iraq — the game has changed. For the first time since the end of World War II, American legitimacy, or the very right to exercise America's power on the world stage and to count on the support of others in doing so, has come under fire. Without legitimacy, it will not be feasible for the United States to make and sustain the alliance relationships that American national security requires. Thus the pursuit of legitimacy must be understood as an instrumental element of alliance policy.

With traditional approaches to prevention, deterrence, and defense under siege, alliances offer a crucial mechanism for working to achieve an updated consensus on when and how to use force. Planning for and using American power in a multinational context provides the single most effective mechanism for ensuring that U.S. actions are perceived to be legitimate. Acting without such international "cover" is increasingly problematic, because it foments resistance to U.S. policies and because the United States needs the help of others to achieve its goals, especially in the arduous and extended aftermath of most military operations. Acting through its alliances, the United States can blunt the hegemonic edge of American leadership, share costs and risks, and increase the prospects of success.

The legitimacy conferred by alliance relationships can either strengthen the U.S. hand or reduce its effectiveness in another way. If America uses its power in ways that are perceived to respect international norms, it can bolster the global stature and influence of its allies. This creates a favorable climate for the pursuit of its national security goals. Conversely, if it chooses to act outside of its alliances, it undermines its allies' international standing, making it harder for them to support American policies. This, in turn, makes it harder to achieve American objectives. Ultimately, the United States also risks diminishing the stature of leaders who are most closely identified with its policies leading to their ouster and the election of governments less committed to cooperation with the United States. Revealingly, President Bush's closest ally in the war on terror, British Prime Minister Tony Blair, has pleaded with the United States to take a more cooperative approach. At the annual Davos conclave in January 2005, he asserted: "If America wants the rest of the world to be part of the agenda it has set, it must be part of their agenda, too."[22]

Averting the Impulse to Counterbalance American Power.

As America's power has become ever more dominant, a growing inclination, even among its closest allies, is to seek means of constraining U.S. unilateralism—to bind the American Gulliver. In the Atlantic Alliance, this is due in part to historical European discomfort with the imbalance of power that rendered the members of NATO largely dependent on America for their security for half a century.[23] The current effort to generate EU foreign and defense policy competencies in part reflects the impulse to create a counterweight. In the U.S.-Korean relationship, a new generation of Koreans now yearns to diminish American influence on regional security affairs and chart its own course, potentially balancing U.S. power through the cultivation of closer relations with China.

Across history, states have formed alliances to enhance their power. The godfather of American realists, Hans Morgenthau, anchored the notion of alliances as force multipliers in the minds of many a national security expert. States act, he contended, based on interests — which largely are motivated by the quest for power and national stature — and therefore seek to establish alliances not as a matter of "principle, but of expediency." By contrast, he argued, a nation will "shun alliances if it believes that it is strong enough to hold its own unaided" or if the obligations of partnership outweigh the benefits.[24]

The idea that alliances contribute to checking the imperial ambition of a nation or group of nations guided mainstream American foreign and defense policy intellectuals for a half-century. It animated the creation of a network of alliance relationships to contain Soviet expansionism in the early 1950s that transformed the U.S. global role. Further, the alliances built during that era provided a firm Western anchor for countries that might otherwise have wavered in their political orientation. They also offered vehicles through which allied militaries developed doctrine, equipped interoperable forces, and conducted continuous combined training. The reality of ongoing military-to-military cooperation between the United States and numerous countries around the world provided a strong deterrent as well as a warfighting capability.

The pernicious power being balanced and contained by the post-World War II American alliance system evaporated nearly 15 years ago, resulting in a unipolar world in which the United States assumed the status of the lone superpower. Until recently, what the French have described as American "hyperpuissance" did not provoke alliance formation to counterbalance this unprecedented strength. The failure to do so can be explained by the fact that states resort to such binding ties that infringe upon their autonomy for the most part only when they perceive they are threatened.[25]

Warning signs abound, however, that perceptions of the United States and its role in the world are shifting from benign to malign. The view that American power presents a challenge to global peace and stability is a relatively new phenomenon. During the Cold War, the United States was the beacon of hope to many living behind the Iron Curtain. In a short period of time, public attitudes—even in countries that have been America's closest allies—have shifted dramatically.[26] The price of such intimate association is perceived to be increasingly costly.

The more disproportionate is America's strength, the more its alliances serve its purposes. The United States needs the support of others to pursue its global goals; as Richard Haass recently wrote in *The Opportunity*, "leadership implies followership."[27] By transmitting its power through binational or multinational structures, America undercuts potential balancing behavior. While the United States may prefer to be unconstrained by obligations to others because it is burdensome to have to accommodate the views of allies or to act in their interest, their cooperation is critical to meeting the security challenges of the 21st century. In this context, shunning alliances is actually contrary to Morgenthau's realist tenets.

Steering Partners away from Strategic Apathy or Excessive Self-reliance.

Another challenge facing the United States is the real danger that key allies will cease to believe that international security requires their active engagement. The end of the Cold War exacerbated latent tendencies in this direction, and the construction of a unified Europe has provided an internally-oriented focal point for many over the past decade. Such a divergence of attention has begun to create a divergence of interests that undermines solidarity in the Atlantic Alliance. Across the globe and under different circumstances, long-standing American ties in the Republic of Korea are facing challenges, especially from those born long after the Korean war who feel no debt to the United States, with the potential to significantly alter the security landscape in that region and beyond.

Historically, American alliances have provided the framework within which the United States and its partners have built a strong foundation of shared values and sustained a constant process of public education that ensured continuing commitments to security cooperation. Among the original members of NATO, democratic institutions and processes have been a common denominator that strengthened their bonds; in cases where democracy has been shaky, U.S. leadership and engagement have provided leverage for democratic progress. Today, the growing ranks of democracies in Europe and Asia provide the most likely pool of allies that have a strong interest in maintaining global stability and an open economic system and can be inspired to retain or embrace a sense of international responsibility that can be translated into concrete capabilities and commitments. In the absence of the continuous political and military coordinating mechanism that effective alliances provide, America cannot assume that other countries will generate or maintain the consensus required to play a constructive global role.

In the other extreme, countries that perceive their vital interests to be threatened but which do not feel confident that their security is embedded in a network of reliable relationships may be inclined to pursue autarkic paths that undermine rather than strengthen international stability. The history of efforts to prevent nuclear proliferation is instructive on this point. A number of key allies—notably Germany and Japan— have benefited from the American nuclear guaranty and have, to date, foregone the development of their own nuclear weapons. This also has reduced stimuli for arms racing among their neighbors and rivals. Further, opportunities to establish cooperative security ties with the United States and NATO during the 1990s generated incentives for complete denuclearization in Ukraine, Kazakhstan, and Belarus. In those three cases, the promise to expand cooperation in the future was a major inducement for doing the right thing at the time. Looking forward, leaders seeking to distance their countries from the United States or feeling insecure about American policies could fan the flames of fanatical nationalism, leading some to revisit and possibly reverse their commitments to the Nuclear Non-Proliferation Treaty.

WHAT ALLIANCES CAN AMERICA COUNT ON TODAY?

In 2006, the landscape of American commitments around the world—as well as the commitments that others have made to the United States—retains many of the features of the Cold War alliance system. In sum, the arrangements are neither systematic nor comprehensive. The durability of the old structures can be explained by several factors: the pent-up longing for association with the West that finally was requited after the collapse of the Union of Soviet Socialist Republics (USSR); the U.S.-led effort to redefine the missions of key alliances and partnerships in the 1990s; sheer inertia; and that 15 years is a mere blip in human history, so that change may be underway but, as yet, is not entirely perceptible, especially because the generation that invested so much in Cold War institutions still retains some influence over the policy process in many allied countries.

Looking at the globe, two major sets of alliance relationships are discernable, one cluster in Europe and one in Asia. They are vastly different in structure and in content. In addition, the United States maintains bilateral alliance relationships with countries in other regions, predominantly in the Middle East. What is most striking is that there is no overarching framework for America's relationships abroad and that unparalleled U.S. power does not translate necessarily into the ability to achieve American security goals. In addition, there are broad swaths of territory across Africa and Latin America where the United States does not have alliances. In the Cold War, security analysts used to worry about a "strategy-force mismatch"; now they at least should be concerned equally about the "power-influence mismatch."

In the taxonomy of American alliance relationships, NATO has been the gold standard. The Article V security guarantee, which requires each member to come to the defense of any other, is without rival. Over its more than 50-year history, NATO has evolved an elaborate set of procedures, supported by a strong institutional framework that has both a political and a military dimension, that has provided the focus and momentum for joint action. Every day in Brussels (NATO's political headquarters), Mons (NATO's military headquarters), and a variety of diplomatic outposts and subordinate commands, the business of the alliance is conducted. Traditionally, an assignment to NATO has been considered to be prestigious and career-enhancing and consequently has been highly sought after by the best and the brightest public servants in allied nations, creating an elite network across all the member countries of individuals who are deeply invested in transatlantic ties.

Adding to its allure and to the swelling of its ranks, NATO adapted to changing times when its long-time "raison d'etre" — the Soviet threat — literally disappeared. With the collapse of the Soviet Union and the dissolution of the Warsaw Pact, a new category of countries emerged on the world stage that for decades had either not existed or did not have the opportunity to choose an orientation or seek a meaningful international role. The United States led a concerted effort in the mid-1990s to establish substantial bilateral security ties with each of these states, as well as between NATO and each of these countries. The implementation of this concept changed the map of Europe, erasing old dividing lines and creating new opportunities for collaboration in pursuit of common security interests.[28]

Asserting its operational relevance, NATO took the bold decision in the mid-1990s to engage in offensive military action for the first time in its history in the former Yugoslavia. In the past few years, it has put to rest the age-old argument about whether it would go "out-of-area" to advance and defend allied interests. While the United States made a mistake in not finding a way to take advantage of NATO's invocation of the Article V guarantee when it went into Afghanistan in the aftermath of 9/11, subsequent efforts to bring NATO into the peacekeeping and reconstruction efforts there and in Iraq have considerably advanced its efforts to achieve consensus on a post-Cold War "out-of-area" role.

Furthermore, the bilateral relationships that undergird NATO are among the strongest in world. Because of historic U.S. leadership of NATO, the ties between each of the now 25 national capitals and Washington have been an important component of the alliance commitment and an axis through which bonds have been cultivated and solidified. The "Special Relationship" between the United States and the United Kingdom has weathered many storms, but to this day the cooperation between the two has unparalleled scope and depth.[29] Other relationships in the "Old Europe" share many of these features, and at times—especially in the case of France—the public expressions of acrimony are in direct proportion to the intensity of cooperation behind the scenes. In addition, for many years a discreet body known as "the Quad" functioned as a kind of steering committee for the Alliance, in which senior political and military officials from the United States, the UK, France, and Germany met regularly to discuss and coordinate policy initiatives. This has fallen into disuse as a consequence of Iraq and because of frustration on the part of other NATO members at being excluded from such an elite club.

A number of new bilateral relationships have emerged over the past 15 years. With the collapse of the Soviet Union in 1991, its 15 constituent republics became independent countries; in addition, the Eastern European countries that had been held hostage by the Communist grip became free to choose their partners. The United States seized the initiative in the last decade of the century to build security cooperation relationships across Eurasia. From Poland to Uzbekistan, leaders chose to establish the most binding ties that the United States was willing to offer; in complement many aggressively sought membership in NATO.

In Asia today, the United States faces an entirely different set of opportunities and challenges to the maintenance of durable security ties. No structure like NATO integrates American allies into a web of relationships or provides the vehicle for day-to-day policy coordination and combined military training that NATO offers. With Australia, Japan, the Philippines, the Republic of Korea, and Thailand, the United States has long-standing bilateral mutual security or defense treaties. Some provide reciprocal security guarantees; some are less explicit in their defense obligations. In the cases of Japan and Korea, the agreements have involved the basing of large numbers of U.S. troops. Pakistan and Thailand also have been designated a "Major Non-NATO Ally," which is a title of uncertain distinction; they have become eligible for certain kinds of military assistance, including purchasing excess defense articles and participating in cooperative defense research and development projects. At last, India appears to be on the cusp of becoming an ally.

Several of these bilateral relationships are under considerable strain. Although some have been strengthened, such as the U.S.-Japan alliance, generational change in which the benefits of partnership with the United States do not have the same valence as they did during the Cold War (and indeed may have negative associations) will inevitably affect future attitudes. Continued fidelity cannot be assumed or assured unless America is effective in revitalizing commitments. Taiwan represents a unique case in which the United States has deterred Chinese aggression through close military cooperation but resists the aggrandizement of this relationship into alliance status.[30]

Although there is no NATO for Asia, there are a number of multilateral groups that address security issues. Some date to the period of "Pactomania" that characterized U.S. policy in the early years of the Cold War. These organizations, Australia-New Zealand-U.S. Treaty (ANZUS) and Southeast Asia Treaty Organization (SEATO), never developed anything parallel to the institutional framework that grew up around the initial NATO commitment, and indeed the command and control apparatus for ANZUS has been largely absorbed by the U.S. Pacific Command. SEATO had no unconditional "attack on one is an attack on all" provision, and is now largely dormant.

Since the end of the Cold War, several new structures have emerged in Asia, some of which involve the United States but several of which pointedly do not. Americans do participate in both Asia-Pacific Economic Cooperation (APEC), which deals principally with economics, and the Association of Southeast Asian Nations (ASEAN) Regional Forum (ARF), a vehicle for security dialogue in the Asia-Pacific region. The newest entrant is the mechanism of the "Six Party Talks" that were established in 2003 to address the security challenge posed by North Korea's nuclear ambitions; these involve the United States, China, Japan, Russia, and both North and South Korea. Washington and

Seoul have expressed joint interest in this becoming a permanent consultative forum. In stark contrast, "ASEAN Plus Three" — a process involving Southeast Asian nations along with China, Japan, and the Republic of Korea — and the Shanghai Cooperation Organization (SCO), which involves China, Kazakhstan, Kyrgyzstan, Russia, Tajikistan, and Uzbekistan (and which recently extended observer status to India, Iran, Mongolia, and Pakistan), do not accord Americans a place at the table.

DO AMERICA'S ALLIANCES MEET U.S. NEEDS?

The array of relationships that exists today provides a strong foundation for the exercise of American influence. However, it needs to evolve in several critical dimensions to meet present and future needs. First, the United States must accept the reality that its allies no longer depend as they once did on the American security guarantee. Second, the United States needs to spearhead a sustained initiative to reconcile the tension between the regional rootedness of its partnerships and the increasingly globalized nature of 21st century security challenges. Third, the United States should work to expand its alliance relationships to encompass a wider set of governmental and nongovernmental capabilities that provide tools to respond to the full range of threats that it will face.

In the 20th century, Europe absorbed the lion's share of America's international energies. Although conflicts in other regions of the world preoccupied the United States from time to time, Europe dominated in terms of the attention and resources it absorbed and the partnership it offered in support of U.S. policies. In the 21st century, other regions of the world command

American interest and engagement. With Europe reunified, "whole and free," the United States is no longer riveted on its fate; so, too, the Europeans feel they no longer need to depend on the United States for their security as they did throughout the Cold War. The same may be said, albeit to a somewhat lesser degree, of American alliances in Asia. Overall, the tables are turning slowly: In the future, the United States—all powerful in one dimension but often hamstrung by its very might—may depend more rather than less on its allies in Europe and Asia to achieve its global goals.

Further challenging existing maps and mindsets, the United States is now faced with the phenomenon of globalization in all its dimensions. Though the most precise definition is an economic one,[31] globalization has significant implications in the security domain, with consequences for threats as well as responses. With respect to alliances, it compels rethinking of some of the fundamentals. In the face of transnational dangers, alliances will need to be defined in broader terms than the classical geographically-based model. Transregional linkages among allies and alliances will need to be forged in response to the fact that many 21st century threats are global rather than regional.

Within this context, effective security cooperation also necessitates a much wider embrace of governmental functions. This is true within the American government, between the United States and key allies, and among alliances that span the globe. Alliances provide the political framework, the fundamental underpinning, to broad engagement across agencies that affect national security. It will be necessary to build up over time, both bilaterally and in multinational alliances, a dense network of interactions. This will be crucial in dealing with threats such as WMD proliferation and stateless terrorism, which are less susceptible to traditional military tools and which instead require intimate cooperation across previously "domestic" structures such as departments of justice, treasury, health, and law enforcement. Old notions of protection of national intelligence assets also are challenged severely by the imperatives of addressing new threats, where the sharing of information on a timely basis may make the difference between life and death for millions.

HOW DOES AMERICA GET THERE FROM HERE?

An American alliance *strategy* would take a comprehensive, long-range view of national security requirements and would be multifaceted, multilayered, and multiyear. It would commit the United States to a four-pronged policy: first, to build upon existing bilateral and multilateral alliance institutions, relationships, and capabilities; second, to promote the establishment of stronger ties that might become enduring alliances (both bilaterally and multilaterally) with several key countries and regions; third, to invest in peacetime security cooperation with countries that can be coaxed toward partnership and may in the future be capable of sustaining an alliance relationship; and fourth, to utilize the full spectrum of cooperative international arrangements that complement alliances.

To follow these simultaneous paths, American policymakers would need to pursue a new approach to the leadership and management of its alliances. Shouldering the preponderance of the burden and wielding proportionate clout is no longer a sustainable posture for the United States; the imbalance of unipolarity requires a shrewder distribution of power and responsibility. To protect and advance American national interests, the United States needs to empower others in order to build and sustain consensus regarding the most challenging security issues of our times.

The hard bargain that would need to be struck would be that America's allies would earn increasing clout as they generate meaningful capabilities and demonstrate a willingness to use them in the face of real threats. Going forward, this would mean that rather than assuming the magnanimous—and sometimes patronizing—role of the guarantor of security in alliance relationships, and assuming that it therefore should be accorded the dominant voice in setting the agenda, in developing policy initiatives, and in deciding on courses of action, the United States explicitly would give allies more voice and more capacity to influence their own future in exchange for their assumption of greater responsibility. In some instances, the United States would delegate power in order to accrue it.

First Prong: Build upon Existing Bilateral and Multilateral Institutions, Relationships, and Capabilities, and Create a Network among Them.

The vitality and magnetism of existing alliance relationships, both bilateral and multilateral, should not be underestimated. The attraction of what during the Cold War was referred to as the "West," as evidenced by the long list of countries still clamoring to get into NATO, is testimony to this fact. Indeed, throughout the administrations of George H. W. Bush and Bill Clinton, American power—and indeed America's status as the lone remaining superpower—generated little antipathy. Instead, countries that had been barred from engagement with the United States leapt at the opportunity to establishing the most binding ties that Washington was willing to offer.

In the aftermath of the first term of George W. Bush, a number of long-standing close allies distanced themselves from the United States. Polling data shows a huge drop in public support for American policies and doubts about America's role in the world. However, goodwill—and a longing to work constructively together—still remains, especially among the older generation that recalls the role America played in ensuring freedom in Europe and Asia and among elites that have much invested in transatlantic ties. For the younger generations, U.S. behavior now and in the near future will influence profoundly whether they see American leadership as benign or malign.

The Bush administration needs to undertake a major effort to renew the most important bilateral relationships. Spanning the globe from Turkey to the Republic of Korea, from Brazil to Poland, a systematic and sustained commitment to listening to allies is required urgently. Consultation must be more than just informing counterparts of predetermined American positions; it must take their perspectives into consideration while policies are being formulated. Genuine give and take is crucial to the achievement of consensus on threats and responses. Furthermore, in numerous cases these bilateral ties also are the essential building blocks of multinational alliances.

Given the pace of globalization and the transnational and transregional nature of new threats, it makes sense to ask whether the existing regionally-based alliance structures are outdated. To a certain extent, geography is still destiny, and the neighborhood in which a state exists will play a great part in shaping its security perspective and in determining its participation in alliances. But to be relevant to the full range of real and potential security challenges, alliances increasingly must be functionally oriented. NATO already has realized this important trend and has transformed itself, moving from a strict definition of its theater of operations to common acceptance that its only meaningful missions will most likely be "out-of-area."

Extending this concept further, NATO should pursue a greater degree of interface and potential formal coordination with other countries, groups, and organizations. Already, some of this is taking place, through mechanisms such as the Istanbul Cooperation Initiative, Mediterranean Dialogue, and Southeast Europe Initiative; in discussions of expanded linkages with Israel; in structured partnerships with Russia and Ukraine; and in dialogues with Australia, Japan, and the Republic of Korea. However, no overarching conceptual framework exists for these arrangements. The evolution of mechanisms for marrying NATO's competencies with the EU potential will be critical in this regard as well, especially as the EU seeks to expand its range of competencies.[32]

In Asia, U.S. interests dictate the maintenance of a robust diplomatic, economic and military presence for many reasons. In the cases of Japan and the Republic of Korea, it is far preferable to wrestle with disagreements within the context of an alliance relationship than to succumb to pressures that would cast either one of them strategically adrift. Further, the presence of U.S. forces in both countries ensures that neither begins to feel that it is isolated in playing its role as an American ally; should the U.S. presence be reduced drastically or terminated in one, pressures could mount in the other to follow suit. As China plays an increasingly shrewd game in the region, cultivating opportunities to enhance its power in ways that may diminish the U.S. role, America's Asian alliances become all the more significant. Furthermore, they are necessary building blocks for collective responses to global security challenges.

Looking to the longer term, the United States should seek to establish a worldwide *network* of key allies, with the objective of establishing an alliance of alliances. This would permit bridge-building between and among existing institutional arrangements, and would facilitate linkages with broader organizations such as the G8, the OSCE and the UN. It would allow each to perform to its competitive advantage, marrying competences in diplomacy, economics, and defense. Such a multiplicity of capabilities is required urgently in meeting threats such as those posed by transnational terrorist groups—threats which require far more extensive and intimate cooperation than the coordination of military action and which themselves exploit the network model. Such an approach also would take advantage of what exists and what does work and avoid having to try to create entirely new institutions when and where that may be too hard or costly in political will, manpower, dollars, or time.

**Second Prong: Promote the Establishment
of Stronger Ties that Have the Potential to Become
Enduring Alliance Relationships.**

A U.S. alliance strategy that maximizes the benefits of enduring security cooperation relationships would not only seek to strengthen existing bilateral and multilateral arrangements but also to advance the development of relationships that currently fall short of alliance status. For a variety of reasons, it will most likely not be realistic to offer or ask for NATO Article V style guarantees, but the United States, nevertheless, can and should pursue the institutionalization of security cooperation with a number of countries.

In identifying countries that should be considered as potential allies, the United States should take into consideration a complex of factors, including governance, geography, regional stature, and potential for meaningful security cooperation. Based on these standards, in the bilateral domain, *primus inter pares* should be the development of fuller security ties with India. With a very capable professional military under firm civilian control—setting it apart from many of its neighbors—and major modernization programs underway, India has the potential to be a highly competent military partner. Much progress has been made in this direction in the past 5 years, but much more is possible. Inevitably the pursuit of enhanced ties with India will complicate the relationship with Pakistan, and while this dynamic must be well-managed, it should not stand in the way of the fruition of an important alliance relationship. Other countries that present opportunities for the advancement of bilateral security cooperation with a view toward the establishment of more formal alliance ties include Brazil, Egypt, Indonesia, Malaysia, and South Africa.

In the multilateral domain, the absence of a security cooperation mechanism is most striking in Asia. The United States has played a major stabilizing role in the region since the end of World War II and has relied heavily on bilateral relationships to achieve its security goals. Historic and current rivalries among regional powers have been a major obstacle to the establishment of institutionalized multinational cooperation. Yet the need is greater than ever for a mechanism that provides a regular forum for consultation, policy coordination, and crisis management and response. Given the nature of the threats, it would be preferable that this mechanism not be narrowly defined in security terms, though it would be optimal if it offered the prospect of combined military capabilities, at least in the peacekeeping domain. Finally, such a mechanism could create a vehicle for policy coordination with institutions in other regions, such as NATO, especially in the face of global threats.

Third Prong: Pursue Peacetime Security Cooperation with Countries that Will Not Necessarily Become Formal Allies.

A much undervalued U.S. policy instrument involves the pursuit of peacetime security cooperation with countries whose orientation and future may be uncertain. Former Defense Secretary William J. Perry described such initiatives as "defense by other means,"[33] suggesting the long-term benefits to national security that they can generate without having to put American soldiers in harm's way. The 2006 *Quadrennial Defense Review Report* provides some guidance in support of this approach. For example, it makes the case for "Security cooperation and engagement activities including joint training exercises, senior staff talks, and officer and foreign internal defense training to increase understanding, strengthen allies and partners, and accurately communicate U.S. objectives and intent."[34] Correctly conceived and executed, such efforts can reduce suspicion, build confidence, and encourage reform; they can also lay the foundations for prospective partnership and potential alliance relationships. In Latin America and Africa, defense cooperation often has followed this looser model; the results have been mixed, but on balance favorable.

Such initiatives are usually low in cost but offer the possibility of big payoffs if they are sound conceptually and pursued with sensitivity and discretion. A leading example took place a decade ago in Central Asia. Looking at maps of the world, senior Pentagon officials noted that what had been considered the underbelly of the Soviet Union was now accessible and without firm geopolitical orientation. A subsequent relatively modest program to establish bilateral and multilateral security ties with these countries literally redefined the borders of Europe so that newly independent states adjacent to Afghanistan and Iran became members of NATO's Partnership for Peace and offered basing rights to the United States after 9/11.

Today, a variety of countries exist in the world with whom discreet, substantive security cooperation—such as in preventing proliferation or interdicting terrorist activity—can contribute to shaping positive perceptions. In some cases, these initiatives will establish patterns of behavior that ultimately might take on the characteristics of an alliance. In others, they may not lead to such close ties but nevertheless will anchor participants in activities that serve their own security interests as well as contribute to American goals, demonstrating the rewards of partnership to both sides. In less felicitous cases, they provide American policymakers with valuable early warning about deteriorating domestic conditions, derailments in bilateral relations, or looming sources of conflict.

Such investments require U.S. policymakers to look beyond the immediate requirements of national security. They require sustained engagement, and taking a genuine interest in the perspectives and concerns of other countries. For the senior leadership in Washington, this kind of work sometimes presents what might be called a problem of "bandwidth," as they are so preoccupied with the crisis of the day that it is hard to make time to do anything where the payoff might not be until a subsequent administration. However, the American government has sufficient capacity to do the job, especially when its policies are clear, and more junior officials are given a mandate to act with authority and some autonomy. The U.S. military can also contribute a great deal in this regard, as it demonstrated in spearheading multiple "shaping" missions during the 1990s.[35]

Fourth Prong: Utilize the Full Spectrum of Cooperative International Arrangements that Complement Alliances.

An effective American alliance strategy would be complemented and indeed strengthened by the recognition that alliances will not fulfill all U.S. national security needs, and that other arrangements may be more appropriate in specific circumstances. The informal approach to multilateralism has sound roots: During the Cold War, for example, the United States and its NATO allies found that out-of-area challenges beyond the formal domain of allied commitment often were best met through ad hoc arrangements. These drew upon the political foundation and military preparedness of the Alliance structure, but did not burden the allies with reaching agreement to or participation in action by all members.[36] A leading contemporary case of such cooperation was the first Gulf War, for which the United States organized a multinational coalition that drew upon NATO assets outside the formal Alliance framework and also involved non-NATO nations. The Combined Joint Task Force model developed in the mid-1990s to create a vehicle for those NATO members with the will and capability to take action beyond the European theater is an example of available synergies between existing alliance structures and less formal arrangements.

In the diplomatic realm, informal coalitions have been devised to address specific policy challenges, and "contact groups" have been created for ongoing conflict resolution efforts such as the Middle East peace process and the status of Nagorno-Karabakh. Further, processes such as the Six Party Talks on North Korea have facilitated engagement with interested parties on an issue of vital national security concern to the United States. Finally, the Proliferation Security Initiative (PSI) has created a new model of cooperation for a specific international security challenge: interdicting the transit of materials and delivery systems for WMD.[37] These examples suggest the range of additional possibilities available to an American administration that seeks to fully exploit opportunities for international support.

Less formal structures do not, however, supplant more formal arrangements. Indeed, the success of informal undertakings will depend in large part on the vitality and durability of the bilateral and multilateral ties the United States maintains and cultivates. Decisions about participation in such ad hoc groupings will continue to be made on a case-by-case basis in national capitals. Further, multilateral alliances can generate momentum and incentives for supporting American initiatives that are being pursued through more informal processes.

CONCLUSION

As the smoke and dust hung heavy over lower Manhattan in the aftermath of 9/11, a headline in the French newspaper, *Le Monde*, announced: "Nous sommes tous Americains."[38] Echoing the sentiment expressed nearly 4 decades earlier by President John F. Kennedy in Berlin, this bold statement underscored the extent to which allies' fates are inextricably intertwined. Such solidarity will again be required to meet the security challenges of the 21st century.

To achieve an enduring sense of common interest and purpose, it will not be sufficient to flex American power and expect others to fall in line. The United States must find ways to transform its power into a magnetic force that draws peoples and nations to its goals. It will not serve American national security interests to disparage multilateralism nor to abandon the pursuit of enduring ties in the illusory hope that less formal arrangements will provide both flexibility and sustained support. The United States must rebuild its alliances and innovate a new kind of connectivity across countries, institutions, and regions that results in a broadly-based alliance system that is far greater than the sum of its disparate parts. The United States also must remain committed to the nitty-gritty effort to make it possible for foreign forces to operate capably alongside American troops, and to establish mechanisms that permit more effective security cooperation with international institutions and nongovernmental organizations (NGOs).

Day in and day out, the default mode must work with allies to get things done. In the short run, it may be easier to go it alone. However, foreign and defense policies are not only measured by how they respond to present requirements, but also by whether they create the conditions for a safer future. A strategic approach to American alliances will enable the United States to translate its unique power into effective global influence that genuinely enhances American national security.

ENDNOTES

1. *Treaties in Force*, published by the U.S. Government, comes closest to being a thorough compilation, but it is so detailed that it offers little perspective on the real utility or relative value of legally binding ties. See Office of the Legal Advisor, *Treaties in Force: A List of Treaties and Other International Agreements of the United States*, Washington, DC: U.S. Department of State, January 1, 2004.

2. Ashton B. Carter, "How to Counter WMD," *Foreign Affairs*, Vol. 83, No. 5, September/October 2004, p. 74.

3. George Washington, "Farewell Address to the People of the United States," *Independent Chronicle*, September 26, 1796; and Thomas Jefferson, "First Inaugural Address," March 4, 1801, *usinfo.state.gov/usa/infousa/facts/democrac/11.htm*.

4. Condoleeza Rice, "Campaign 2000: Promoting the National Interest," *Foreign Affairs*, Vol. 79, No. 1, January/February 2000, pp. 46-47.

5. Ivo H. Daalder and James M. Lindsay, *America Unbound: The Bush Revolution in Foreign Policy*, Washington, DC: Brookings Institution Press, 2003, pp. 40-45.

6. Rice, "Promoting the National Interest," pp. 47-48.

7. *Ibid.*, p. 62.

8. Governor George W. Bush, "A Distinctly American Internationalism," Ronald Reagan Presidential Library, November 19, 1999, *www.mtholyoke.edu/acad/intrel/bush/wspeech.htm*.

9. Paul Wolfowitz, "Remembering the Future," *The National Interest*, Vol. 59, Spring 2000, p. 41.

10. Richard Haass, *The Reluctant Sheriff: The United States After the Cold War*, New York: Council on Foreign Relations, 1997, pp. 78-80.

11. See NATO doctrine on Combined Joint Task Forces at *www. nato.int/docu/facts/2000/cjtf-con.htm*.

12. Haass, *The Reluctant Sheriff,* pp. 93-97.

13. Bob Woodward, *Bush at War,* New York: Simon & Schuster, 2002, p. 281.

14. Secretary of Defense Donald Rumsfeld, interview by Larry King, *Larry King Live,* CNN, December 5, 2001.

15. President George W. Bush, "State of the Union Address," January 20, 2004.

16. See, for example, Wesley K. Clark, *Waging Modern War,* New York: Public Affairs, 2001.

17. See, for example, U.S. Department of Defense, *Report to Congress, Kosovo/Operation Allied Force After-Action* Report; Benjamin S. Lambeth, *The Transformation of American Air Power,* Ithaca, NY: Cornell University Press, 2000, p. 213; and James P. Thomas, *The Military Challenges of Transatlantic Coalitions,* Adelphi Paper No. 333, London: International Institute for Strategic Studies (IISS), May 2000, p. 53.

18. Charles Krauthammer, "Who Needs Allies?" *Time International,* January 26, 2004.

19. See, for example, Secretary of State Condoleezza Rice, "Remarks at the Institut d'Etudes Politiques," Paris, France, February 8, 2005; and President Bush, "Second Inaugural Address," Washington, DC, January 20, 2005.

20. Ariel E. Levite and Elizabeth Sherwood-Randall, "The Case for Discriminate Force," *Survival,* Vol. 44, No. 4, Winter 2002-03.

21. David C. Gompert, Richard L. Kugler, and Martin C. Libicki, *Mind the Gap,* Washington, DC: National Defense University Press, 1999; and Elizabeth Sherwood-Randall, "Managing the Pentagon's International Relations," in Ashton B. Carter and John P. White, eds., *Keeping the Edge: Managing Defense for the Future,* Cambridge: MIT Press, 2000, pp. 235-264.

22. Blair, quoted in Robert Wielaard, "Blair: U.S. Needs to Integrate With World," Associated Press, January 26, 2005.

23. For an insightful and enduring treatment of the challenge that America's unrivaled power poses to its foreign policy, see Stanley Hoffmann, *Gulliver's Troubles, Or the Setting of American Foreign Policy,* New York: McGraw Hill, 1968.

24. Hans Morgenthau, *Politics Among Nations: The Struggle for Power and Peace*, 5th ed., New York: Knopf, 1978, p. 181.

25. Stephen M. Walt, *The Origins of Alliances*, Ithaca: Cornell University Press, 1987, p. 5.

26. See surveys: "A Year After Iraq War: Mistrust of America in Europe Even Higher," Pew Research Center, March 16, 2004, *pewglobal.org/reports/pdf/206.pdf*; "Transatlantic Trends 2004," German Marshall Fund, September 9, 2004, *www.transatlantictrends. org/apps/gmf/ttweb2004.nsf*; "Transatlantic Trends: Key Findings 2005," German Marshall Fund, September 7, 2005, *www. transatlantictrends.org/doc/TTKeyFindings2005.pdf*; and "America's Image Slips, But Allies Share U.S. Concerns Over Iran, Hamas," in Pew Global Attitudes Project, June 13, 2006, *pewglobal.org/reports/ pdf/252pdf*.

27. Richard Haass, *The Opportunity*, New York: Public Affairs, 2005, p. 26.

28. For example, animated by the Pentagon but under Partnership for Peace (PFP) auspices, a pathbreaking military exercise program led by the then Supreme Allied Commander Atlantic—a strapping U.S. Marine Corps General—conducted joint training in Central Asia among troops of the U.S. 82nd Airborne Division and soldiers from Kazakhstan, Kyrgyzstan, and Uzbekistan. At the time, skeptics thought that security cooperation with this largely forgotten corner of the world, that had been the underbelly of the Soviet Union, would not tangibly benefit the United States. After 9/11, these countries immediately stepped forward to offer their full support in the campaign to rout al-Qai'da and oust the Taliban from neighboring Afghanistan.

29. For a reflection on the history of close U.S.-UK ties by an experienced British participant, see Lord Renwick of Clifton, "Can the 'Special Relationship' Survive Into the 21st Century?" The British Library, October 4, 1998, *www.bl.uk/pdf/renwick.pdf*.

30. Section 3302 of the 1979 Taiwan Relations Act states that:

> The President is directed to inform the Congress promptly of any threat to the security or the social or economic system of the people on Taiwan and any danger to the interests of the United States arising therefrom. The President and the Congress shall determine, in accordance with constitutional processes, appropriate

action by the United States in response to any such danger.

"Taiwan Relations Act of 1979," *U.S. Code* 22, ch. 48, §3302.

31. Martin Wolf, *Why Globalization Works*, New Haven and London: Yale University Press, 2004, p. 13-19.

32. A number of useful ideas for linking the United States, NATO, and the EU are offered by Charles Grant and Mark Leonard in "What New Transatlantic Institutions?" Centre for European Reform Bulletin, Issue 41, April/May 2005, *www.cer.org.uk./articles/41_grant_leonard.html.*

33. See Elizabeth D. Sherwood, "Revolution and Evolution in Russia, Ukraine and Eurasia," *Defense '95*, No. 6, p. 22.

34. *Quadrennial Defense Review Report*, February 6, 2006, Washington, DC: U.S. Department of Defense, p. 31, at *www.dod.mil/pubs/pdfs/QDR20060203.pdf.*

35. In its most recent statement of doctrine, the U.S. military reconfirmed the centrality of this mission to the achievement of U.S. national security goals:

> A deep understanding of the cultural, political, military, and economic characteristics of a region must be established and maintained. Developing this understanding is dependent upon shared training and education, especially with key partners, and may require organizational change as well. The overall effectiveness of multinational operations is, therefore, dependent on interoperability between organizations, processes, and technologies.

Joint Vision 2020, www.dtic.mil/jointvision/jvpub2.htm, pp. 17-18.

36. Elizabeth D. Sherwood, *Allies in Crisis: Meeting Global Challenges to Western Security*, New Haven and London: Yale University Press, 1990, pp. 184-187.

37. See *www.state.gov/t/np/c10390.htm* for further information about PSI.

38. Jean-Marie Colombani, "Nous sommes tous Americains," *Le Monde*, September 12, 2001.